SPORTS PSYCHOLOGY
& All Round Development

Veena Verma

SPORTS PUBLICATION

7/26, Ground Floor, Ansari Road,
Darya Ganj, New Delhi-110002
Phones: (Office) 65749511 (Fax) 011-23240261
(Mobile) 9868028838 (Residence) 27562163
E-mail: lakshaythani@hotmail.com

Published by:

SPORTS PUBLICATION
7/26, Ground Floor, Ansari Road, Darya Ganj, New Delhi-110002
Ph. : (Office) 65749511, 23240261 (Mobile) 9868028838
     (Residence) 27562163 (Fax) 011-23240261
E-mail: *lakshaythani@hotmail.com*

I.S.B.N. – 81-86190-70-8

PRINTED IN INDIA 2009

Laser Typeset by:

JAIN MEDIA GRAPHICS,
C-4/95-A, Keshav Puram, (Lawrence Road), Near Wazirpur Depot,
Delhi-110035. Tel.: 011-20296366, (M) 9911151534, 9350556511

Printed by:

CHAWLA OFFSET PRINTERS
Delhi-110052

Price: Rs. 195/-

ACKNOWLEDGEMENT

I would like to express my sincere thanks

FOR THE CO-OPERATION OF

Mr. Vijay Verma (Deputy Govt. Adv. Supreme Court of India)
Master Tarun Verma
Mr. Sony Takkar
Mrs. Simi Takkar

FOR THE BLESSING OF

Sant Jagan Nath Gothi

FOR THE GUIDANCE OF

Mr. K.K. Gothi (Scientific Officer, R.C.R. brit C/o INMAS, Delhi-54)
Mr. Lokesh Thani (Prop. Sports Publication, Delhi-110 052)
Mr. Deepak Gothi (Prop. Daily Bandematram, Delh-110 053)
Mr. Dilber Gothi

DEDICATED TO

My parents, all my family members and in fond rememberance of my respected Father-in-law **Late Shri Bishandas Verma**.

Veena

CONTENTS

Preface

Till now I have been writing Articles and Poems for my students, Geet and Bhajans for my own self- satisfaction and stories and plays for magazines. First time I have written a small book on sports psychology which I am sure will be of great help to my students who have keen interest in sports too.

It is my personal experience that teaching now-a-days is incomplete without sports. With the help of certain games we can give better understanding of different subjects to our students. Research work is being done in Delhi University which has proved that if we want better results in the tough subjects like Economics, Commerce, Science etc. then we must take the help of games and sports. Any topic of any subject, if taught not only to the primary students but also to the students of senior secondary classes also, has shown everlasting memory effect on the children.

Recently I have attended one seminar in Delhi University and I am highly impressed by research work under the topic:

"Sports psychology and the achievement of
better results in different subjects."

My all best wishes with them who are doing
Action Research in this field.

"Have Sportsman spirit is
        a commonly used phrase,
which means be strong,
        determined and do not
loose any of the life's phase."

"With the help of sports psychology
        we can achieve all round.
development of the child,
        As it fixes the right goals of life,
and stops the children from being wild."

"Sports psychology helps the
        sports teacher to develop
his team with best athletic qualities,
        As sports have a wide range of
special activities which are
        used efficiently to develop the
children in all totalities."

Veena

1
Scientific Study of Sports Psychology in Behaviour and Development

The scientific study of child behaviour and development may be traced to an article "Biographical sketch of an infant by the great British Biologist Charles Darvin (1802-1882) published in 1877. Accordingly, the facts of child behaviour and development were gathered by systematic observation of the growth of children by William Preyer in Germany and Starley Hall in America.

Scientific observation is not only accurate, it also includes the negative findings, the instances which do not fit our expectations. Scientific observation leads to the formation of hypothesis. The writings of the ancients contain questions that are still of interest to contemporary psychologists. The great literature of Greece and Rome contains

1

numerous references to mind-body relationships and questions about the nature of thought, perception, the will and the human mind. Throughout the seventeenth century and into the eighteenth, ideas that were early reflections of such contemporary psychological topics as motivation, perception, intelligence and effort activation were expanded on in departments of philosophy, theology, rhetoric and logic but the philosophical utterences. That appear nebulous today are cited out even then for more precise delineation. Thus the science of mathematics, physics and biology merged in ways that produced the beginning of modern psychology.

The aim of scientific study is to make observations that lead to accurate predictions. Participation in games and sports in the contemporary times has become more comparing with developed scientific knowledge, skills and methods, alongwith the equipment and applied research in the fields, disciplines envisaging applied research in the fields, disciplines envisaging vital alterations to our sedentary life styles. Life and living here progressed in different fields with technological innovations and one finds oneself living in a vying society, facing challenges at every step. In sports too challenges are faced by every nation in the International competitions.

Science of Sports has enabled the today's generation to develop physical capacities. Physical development includes muscular development, mental development and emotional development. All round development includes all the aspects of different types of development. All round development becomes more realistic and practicable with the concept of sports-psychology. A person with great interest in sports develops in all the fields . For example, being a person of sports abilities, he is more capable than others in all tne spheres of life.

Life is full of challenges. So sports psychology helps a person to accept tne challenges smilingly. Life is full of problems. So sports psychology helps a person to face all the problems boldly.

Learning is the life-long process and it includes a wide range of activities. Development of the motor learning and its significance in the educational process in terms of applications to teaching and coaching situations is beyond doubt. Learning does not even have to be intentional. It is demonstrated under such diverse conditions as performing athletic skills, remembering past situations, liking or disliking and belongingness and believing in the team. The research findings indicate that a high level of technique perfection has little to do with the success in the competitive sports if it is restricted by physiological or psychological limits. as most of the sports activities require greater amount of speed. Strength, endurance, flexibility, co-ordinations along with the will power, tolerance power, intellect and mental toughness. The world of sports intrigued the areas of sports sciences concerning bio-mechanics, physiology, sports-medicine and sports psychology as well as the application of practical methods.

2

"SOCIALISATION AND SPORTS PSYCHOLOGY"

Man is the Social animal. Socialisation gives rise to various types of societies. Socialisation covers many good qualities which can easily be grown with the help of sports. In otherwords, sports can lead to better socialisation of different societies.

Today's world knows the importance of sports. Sports psychology helps a person to grow physically brave, mentally strong, emotionally balanced, economically well to do and socially a good name and respect etc.

Socialisation is directly co-related with sports-psychology. At home when children play together they become social and when they go to school, their teaching period does not make them social as their games-period. They come close through games only. When they play together then only they learn to be social also.

Sports and games either in the school system or at home explore the children to many situations and themes.

An experiment was done at Bombay by one Educational Institution in 1991. They opened two Schools together at one time. One school was without sports and the other was with all sports activities. It was found that children of the school where no sports were introduced were not as social as those who were from the School with sports.

Similar experience we can have in a family. If there are two children— one who has interest in games, grows socially sound and the one who doesn't play with others, does not have good social qualities. He becomes introvert, shy and absent mined. A social child is always co-operative, extrovert, intelligent and solves his problems by being resourceful in any situation.

A sports-teacher in the School organises different types of games and involves all the children inclusive children play who are weak in studies. When all children play together they become friendly and when they become friendly they help each other, they love each other and they develop the feeling of unity and belongingness. In this way, weak children work hard in studies and show good results. A child who gets recognition in games, automatically improves in studies also.

Thus, it is true to say that through sports we can achieve better socialisation and better results. A man's personality and his traits are greatly influenced by the social and cultural factors. He is influenced by the beliefs and values of the group in which he/she is brought up.

"As Socialisation is very important for all societies to develop, it is achieved by the help of sports to go up."

The expectations and demands of the various social groups which are of significance to the individual, influence his behaviour.

When a child enters the school, he has to play the role of student, friend etc. If he is elected the leader of the class then he has to play that role also to represent his class with honour. Generally it is seen that the children who are good in sports, only become the leaders and develop special traits in comparison to rest of the children in the class.

It is also observed that in a class of 40 children only 6 or 7 children have interest in sports. So those who are gifted with the sports ability become the example for others.

Role of Social Approval

In sports not only children but adults also need the social approval. When they show achievements, they are encouraged by the words – Buck-up, keep-it-up, get it – you will get it etc. So this type of social approval by coaches, parents, team-mates and spectators attribute virtuous intent to him rather than focus on the goals of competitive ability or sport mastery. This form of achievement goal also focuses upon effort. Usually the approval of the coach is perceived to be dependent upon effort.

To the athlete, trying hard and obtaining coach approval becomes the criterion of success and failure. Similarly social-reinforcement also increases the strength of a response. The teacher who says "very good" or "well-done" after every performance by every student may create a positive, humanistic environment. Elementary school children show greater improvements in performance when social reinforcement is administered by people of opposite sex.

Performing an activity in the presence of others, could be harmful or beneficial. Social psychologists have been interested in the impact of what is referred to as social presence upon performance.

3

EMERGENCE OF SELF AND SPORTS PSYCHOLOGY

The individual's self concept is the picture of himself. It is his view of himself. It is his view of himself as distinct from how he is viewed by other persons on the basis of his behaviour. The term personality refers to a person's behaviour and characteristics which are observed by others. We can observe his personality in different situations. Whether he is tough or emotionally sensitive, whether he is relaxed or tense, whether he is dominant or submissive, whether he is independent and acts on his own, or is dependent on others, whether he conforms to social demands or is a non-conformist. The proper reading of the personality can be done only through sports.

In the schools this particular job is assigned to sports teacher only to give the report on the personality of the children. So sports psychology helps the sports teacher to come out with accurate reading of the personality of the different children.

The self-concept is the individual's anticipation regarding the way in which he is accepted or rejected by other persons who are significant. When the self-concept is formulated it tends to shape his farther behaviour which may confirm to the established pattern. Behaviour then becomes an attempt to maintain the self-concept. The self concept, thus is what a person believes about himself and it enters into his decisions and gives them some consistency. Much of a person's behaviour is an attempt to maintain the consistency of his self-concept. It is shaped with the help of sports activities from early childhood onwards. It depends through his interactions with other people and his environment. It is based on his evaluation of himself and on the evaluation of others. It is a composite of a person's thoughts and feelings, striving and hopes, fear, fantasies and his attitudes pertaining to his worth. Self-awareness is a growth process which develops with the help of sports psychology.

A child of sports always have more adequate self-concept whereas a child without sports activities have poor self-concept.

Sports psychology develops the following aspects of self among the children:

(1) Self-Awareness

The children who participate in games are more conscious about their self in comparison to those who do not participate in sports. When children win the game they get pleasure and when they loose it, they feel irritation, so going through sports activities self awareness can be increased which can make the children more competitive.

(2) Self-Acceptance

Self understanding and self-acceptance are closely associated and contribute to mental health and good inter personal relations. Self-acceptance requires a perception of one's assets and limitations. It is a comparative use of his abilities; whether they are high or low.

When children won or loose the game, their self-acceptance is promoted, their tolerance lead them towards more hard efforts to achieve their target to win the game. They can recognise their own shortcomings and strive for self-improvement.

Self-acceptance promotes self-evaluation. Such a person can be critical about himself and has a sense of responsibilities for his actions. He does not blame others or destiny for his failure but promises himself for more and more hard work to reach his height of expectations.

(3) Self Esteem

Self-esteem is personal judgement of one's worth which is expressed in the attitudes, the individual holds towards himself. Sports individual always have high self esteem. And the persons without sports background lack at sports psychology, they have low self-esteem and lack trust in themselves. They are always afraid at exposing themselves. They listen rather than participate in the game.

4

EMOTIONAL DEVELOPMENT AND SPORTS PSYCHOLOGY

Emotions are the feelings which we are experiencing constantly inside ourselves. Emotions are a natural phase which have a great importance in life.

Love, anger, fear, hatred, wonder etc. are called the emotions. Sometimes due to these emotions we feel pleasant and at the other time these emotions make us feel unpleasant.

In our society, sports only provide us ample opportunities to free ourselves to enjoy pleasurable excitement which are readily available. Among all the living beings, human beings only like to feel competent and self-determining. They achieve great satisfaction which comes from the actual experience of being competent. Emotion is a psychic and physical reaction. It is generally defined in terms

14

of subjective experience of feelings, goal directed behaviours, expressive and physiological arousal. For example, setting target and achieving, smiling, snarling, heart rate increases, sweating etc.

Competition, victory, failure, struggle are the elements of sports activities, which always teach the players to be emotionally balanced. The best, most consistent and most confident performers are able to control or channel their emotions, to focus their concentration and to bounce back from setbacks in an emotionally mature or constructive way. It is very important for top sportsmen to be mentally strong. Ones recognition of the importance of self control, both tactical and emotional, alongwith ones conscientious attempt to maintain and continually improve self control, allowed one to attain a world ranking in his sport and believes will enable him/her to excel even further in the future.

Thoughts can influence emotions and emotions can influence thoughts. The youngsters may develop athletic skills for personal motives and may have the ideal temperament to cope with challenges, frustrations, time spent in practice and other consideration association with preparing for and being involved in sport. A well controlled emotional person has the ability to quickly shift from an emotional reaction to performance focus, particularly in response to increase anxiety or errors. Constructive reaction to errors is a learned process. Well controlled individual can avoid emotional behaviour. Competitive sports for children constitute both positive and negative experiences. Some theories of emotions focus on the relationship between the bodily states in emotion and the emotion as it is felt. In other words, the bodily changes do not cause the felt emotion, while same time, they are independent of each other. Emotional behaviour and emotional awareness are accompanied by physiological events, many of which are mediated by the autonomic nervous system.

Behavioural Approach and Sports Psychology

Teacher and coaches spend a great deal of time keeping scores, evaluating performance, providing feed back and generally reinforcing and punishing behaviour of sport-participants. Behaviour are strengthened when they are rewarded and weakened when they are punished or unrewarded. Good behaviours should be positively reinforced as often as possible and bad behaviour should be ignored most of the time. Punishment should be applied only to behaviour that are intolerable such as behaviour that are dangerous or descriptive to the entire group.

Self confidence in emotional development and sports psychology —

In the process of coaching, coaches should learn to recognise athlete's emotions. The coach should be able to predict how the person is feeling based on the attributions the athlete hides emotions from the athlete emotion's emotional responses. Self-confidence is exhibited by participants in the selectivity, intensity and persistency they exhibit in sport and physical activity. Feeling of self-confidence arises from emotional arousal also.

5

MORAL DEVELOPMENT AND SPORTS PSYCHOLOGY

Physical Development, Mental Development, Motor Development, Social Development, Emotional development– all these developments are important for the all round development of children. But without moral development it is just to say a body fully developed without the development of it's soul or consciousness.

Sports teach us a number of moralities. For e.g. discipline, perfection, enthusiasm teamspirit, principles, rules and regulations, cleanliness of body and mind, etc. are the moral values which can be developed more accurately with the help of sports psychology.

A case-study reveals the relation between moral development and sports psychology and shown how sports and games make the children strong and brave to face and fight with any sort of situation.

Case History and Sports Psychology

Usha was a student of IXth class and she was victimised by her parents. Her mother died when she was only 5 years old. Her father married once again and at present her step mother was torturing her and father was not taking care of her. Usha was very intelligent but her parents did not want her to study further. She was very good at sports also, so she came to me and wept bitterly and told her whole story to me. Being the sports teacher I encouraged her and said "Usha, though you have got challenges at an early age but being a sports girl, you should not loose your heart and be determined that you have to study further and you have to face your parents boldly." Usha smiled and promised to face every situation. I advised her to come in the evening for the extra coaching of Basket-Ball as she was good at this game and had interest in T.T. also. Within six months she became the champion of Basketball and Table Tennis. She started playing at district as well as at state level also She started getting scholarship, so now her parents stopped grumbling for her further studies. I kept on patting her by saying "Buck-up Usha, Buck-up and keep it up."

So, that small frustrated Usha of IXth class is today a Ist class I.A.S. Officer and never forgets to touch my feet and says "Madam it was you and my sports psychology gave me the courage to fight with my terrible condition."

Like wise the sports psychology helps the problem children also.

Nisha was a handicapped girl. She had weak legs and could not walk properly. Her anxiety helped her to overcome her weakness. I placed her seat in the playground and made her to watch the races regularly. When other girls were running I kept on provoking her, come on, Nisha you can also walk, you can also run. You have to strengthen your legs by your strong will power.

So at last my dreams came true and I saw that weak Nisha participating in 100 m. race, then 200 m. race and then 400 m., and then

800 m. Though she was not at Ist place but her participations was a good response to the sports psychology.

Generally, it is observed that those students who are good in sports are all round students. They are good at studies also and are known for their active participation in all curricular activities.

Thus, the importance of sports psychology is closely related with the all round development of children. In short, we may sum up sports as a game which give pleasure to the children. Sports helps in the social development as they play in groups. Sports help them to develop the traits like, helping, co-operation, team-spirit, belonging-ness to the group concerned, leadership etc. Sports keep the children to face all types of challenges. Sports help the children to be bold, to overcome shyness and to be smart. Sports teach them to be emotionally balanced. Sports make the children mentally strong and intelligent.

6

"MOTIVATION AND SPORTS PSYCHOLOGY"

Motivation means any idea, need, emotions or organic state which prompts a man to an action. Motivation plays a major role in the all round development of a child. Sports activities have a higher degree of motivation or in other words through games we can motivate children for better understanding of different aspects of life. Motive is an internal factor that interferes with man's behaviour. Motivation is a process of getting the needs of the people realised with a view to induce them to work or the accomplishment of the task.

Motivation can be defined as a psychological and physical condition that cause one to expend effort to satisfy needs and wants. It is possible that the repetitive presentation of drills over the course of a teaching gear or coaching season might not detract from participant's performance because other motivational factors are undoubtedly in operation. For example, those individuals with exceptional intrinsic motivation or a high need for achievement or those individuals or a good goal setting programme or receiving token rewards might maintain sufficient motivation for effective performance. But there is no doubt that in the general case monotony of routine and a repetition on approach will detract from motivation. Having another person teach your class or coach your team occasionally is also a good idea. Sometimes changing the place of practice also positively effect the motivation of the student.

As a teacher need to motivate his student for studies in the same way a coach also need to motivate his team of players. The sources of potential motivation for the participation in sports and physical activity may be as identifying of the right kind of motives and rewards act as a motivator.

In the schools and colleges scholarships also act as motivator. Competition among students and players also acts as a strong motivator. In the same way knowledge of results and feed back also works as a motivator.

Goal setting and sense of achievement are also strong motivators.

Cognitive aspect of motivation is the perceived ability of the athlete related to the outcome which is attributed to some courses. Some athletes are more successful than others in learning and mastering skills, as in achieving in competition. It is because they control and direct cognitive process through the use of appropriate strategies. Successful athletes have been characterised by their ability to use cognitive strategies effectively. A sensation on the other hand involves the means for the interpretation of stimuli.

Perceptual learning has been studied separately from learning in general, but there is no doubt that although one refers to the learning of athletic skill as motor learning. Perceptual mechanism operate in precluding and skilled motor act or subsequent to that act. Cognition consists of such higher mental processes or concept formation, problem solving, imagination, perception and intelligence.

In order to understand the motivation and subsequent achievement behaviour of individuals in any content, it is necessary to understand the subjective meaning of achievement to the achiever. It is assumed that whether a person demonstrates motivation in any competitive context depends upon the achievement goal of the athlete. And athlete may have many achievement goals, not just one that operate in a given situation. Consequently, when members of athletic teams enter into sport-settings with these different goals, their individual competition of success and failure will differ too. Some may be pleased with winning while others may be pleased with another outcomes such as pleasing the coach, pleasing the team-mate of opposite sex etc.

Motivation is a term which is used to represent the selectivity, the intensity and the persistence which is present in behaviour. Self-confidence may be viewed as a major components of motivation. Self-confidence is exhibiting by participants in the selectivity, intensity and persistence then exhibited in sport and physical activity.

Praise and support are the positive motivators which can be given for the demonstration of desirable behaviours and for non-desirable ones, punishment or non-attention may be the effective motives. Another behavioural dimension underlying motivation is related to the reason children give to explain their success and failure. The child with mastery orientation style attributes personal failure to not enough effort. The result is to try even harder the next time when effort is valued.

It is true to say that an optimal level of motivation is required for better performance. High level of motivation leads to involvement in the activity understanding the reason being participation will enhance levels of performance. For effective use of motivation we should consider the nature of activity and the nature of the learner.

Thus, we may conclude to say that with the help of sports activities we can motivate not only children, but all human beings to get them for a desired work.

7

NATIONAL/INTERNATIONAL INTEGRATION AND SPORTS PSYCHOLOGY

As we all know that India is a country of various castes and creeds. In order to achieve higher degree of unity in diversity, sports play a major role in bringing all together under the feeling of oneness.

Through games when the traits of co-operation, belongingness, love, affection, attachment develop strongly in the children, then automatically we march towards National Integration. Various matches among different States bring the people of different castes and religion close to each other. They not only learn the brotherhood but also gain knowledge of a number of good values of all the religions which gives them a good moral character also. They love and respect other's religions also as they respect their own. They treat all human beings equally.

Thus we can say that sports psychology helps not only children but the nation as a whole.

In the same way when different nations arrange games and sports at international level, their aim is also to improve the relations among different countries. To strengthen the international relations, not only competitive but friendly matches are also being played amongst different countries.

India has developed and improved its relations with Asian and European countries. Through games and sports also India has got good name and recognition in the international world. Games like Cricket and Hockey has made India an outstanding feature of the world.

We all know that Asian Games are being organised by the Asian countries with a view to bring Asian countries close to each other and to develop friendly relations for the progress of the newly developing countries.

All the developing countries need the help and support of big nations. Sports psychology help them to gain warm and friendly help. It is because when two nations come close through games and sports, then they discuss and realise the problems and difficulties of each other. In this way they sign friendly ties and develop their trade and commercial activities by signing treaties.

8

TEACHING AND
SPORTS PSYCHOLOGY

Sports psychology is becoming very popular in the modern trend of education also. As teaching includes the aspects of learning and understanding, Investigators have proved that sports psychology makes the teaching more easy and interesting.

Teaching alone becomes bore and difficult. But if we take the help of sports psychology we can make it easily understandable for the students. Now-a-days for the tough subjects like commerce and economics, the educationalists are taking the help of sports psychology. They have tried it by doing the practical surveys in different schools.

At Central Institute of Education, University of Delhi, it is learnt that few reports have been submitted by the research scholars on "teaching with help of sports psychology. "They have selected certain topics and prepared games for those topics. For example, topic was "Nature of goods" and they prepared a game for this topic through which students understand the topic in a short time. It has been found that particular topic/chapter which is taught with the help of games was liked very much by the students. At the same time the said topic/chapter was taught by the subject teacher with the help of lecture-method. The students of that section who were taught by the game method gave much better response. And after two months when to check the truancy of the topic, it has been found that the students of that section who were taught by lecture-method, could not recall the topic/chapter whereas the students of that section who were taught by the game-method could recall the topic very easily.

Thus, it has been proved that game-method gives better understanding to the students.

Teaching through games is becoming popular not only in primary standard but also in

Secondary/ Sr. Secondary standards for the following reasons:

(i) For better retention;

(ii) For better remembrance for a longer period;

(iii) For difficult topic to make them easy; and

(iv) It automatically creates interest in the students as game is the basic instinct of everyone.

Now-a-days research is going on for "Progressive methods of Teaching." I am sure that for this research "Teaching though the games" will certainly help in achieving the goal.

The main objectives of these methods are:

i) Involvement of the students should be more and more.

ii) Games are the best method of each and every child's *active involvement.*– We can achieve the active involvement of the students by giving directions, by motivating, by communicating and by supervision.

All individuals have three types of activities:

i) Cognitive activities which are related to brain. They are mental activities.

ii) Affective activities include appreciation, encouraging etc.

iii) Psycho-motor activities include hard work.

All these activities can better by learnt through games. For inculcating different types of traits in the students, we use games.

Action Research

For applying it for solving the problems in the schools, action research is going on at C.I.E., University of Delhi. When a teacher enters in the class room, he/she may use:

a) In basket exercises, or

b) Brain storming for quick decision taking.

For such games he has to make a list of questions from the topic and with active involvement of the students, the tough chapters/ topics can be made easily understandable to the students.

Thus, in the end we can say that sport psychology is very important for better teaching.

9

PERSONALITY DEVELOPMENT AND SPORTS PSYCHOLOGY

All individuals love to have a good personality. Personality doesn't mean only physical outlook. Personality development is a very wide term. It includes physical, mental, emotional and social aspects in it.

It is the task of the parents and teachers to understand the facts which are operating on the child and to help him to grow into a complete personality.

Parental love is the vital factor in the personality development of their child. Over protection may lead to a sense of irresponsibility and lacks of self control. Too much of praise and over indulgence are as harmful as neglect and rejection of the child. Similarly, lack of consistent discipline is as harmful as overstrict discipline.

The parents who have achieved a place of distinction may push the child to attain a specific goal though he may not have the necessary ability of the desire for such attainment. In the same way the poor parents may push the child hoping that he will become a highly educated person and earn considerable wealth an enable them to get rid of their poverty.

When the child goes to the school, there is an opportunity for a reformulation of his personality. The school and its playground provides the child with a new setting which operates under new conditions. The child not only gets academic instruction in the school but gets opportunities for social learning. In words a good classroom provides all the characteristics of a good personality for the children.

The Characteristics of the adequate personality and the inadequate personality

Adequate personalities are those who (1) perceive themselves in essentially positive ways, (2) are capable of acceptance of self and others and (3) perceive themselves as closely identified with others.

A person with adequate personality is not compelled to defend himself. He can assess himself. He can himself honestly, accurately and objectively. He takes a problem solving attitude towards the difficult situation he has to face. As a result a child with an adequate original. He trusts himself and others. He is free from negative anticipations.

By contrast the child who has developed an inadequate personality feels insecure and is obsessed by feelings of inferiority. He tends to think of himself as an unwanted, unacceptable and incompetent person. He lacks the courage to meet the life's tasks. Similar traits are to be found in the delinguents and those with disturbed personalities.

Thus, the children who desire to do something worthwhile and productive, they do not look for material rewards nor for praise from others but the satisfaction of attaining their own goals and meeting their own standards for achievement. A responsible personality is one who does his work without being watched or coerced by someone else.

Realising one's potential as a unique human .being is considered a positive, constructive and realistic process.

In the development of the personality of a child, there are two forces — the organism and the environment.

The human infants does not posses a personality at birth, it has only potentiality for developing a personality. As the various structures like the receptors, muscles, brain and nervous system mature and with interaction with the mother and the other persons around him personality emerges as an organization of personal meaning through learning.

Each personality is unique as it develops on the basis of a unique organism and the reactions to the various forces in the social and physical environment. There is a constant and continuous activity of adjustment and readjustment to the changing conditions.

Thus, there is a stability as well as change in the personality. Right through the growth, process in all the physical, physiological, and psychosocial aspects, the personality is a constant but ever growing, ever changing organisation.

Change in personality is revealed in the changes in the ways one seems oneself and the world as one acquires knowledge, skills, attitudes and roles. Perception plays a central role in the development and adjustment of their personality.

There is an increasing awareness of one's personality as the child grows up into adolescene and mature adulthood. Now-a-days each and every individual either he or she are aware of having a good personality.

Sports - Psychology is providing sufficient methods and methodologies for a good personality development. For example, increase in the number of health-centres, sports-centres, aerobics-centres, keep-fit centres, etc.

Thus, sports are becoming very popular as a part and parcel of every personality. We can say that in the coming phase of life, sports psychology will play an important and distinguished role in all the spheres of life.

10

COMPETITION AT DIFFERENT AGE LEVELS AND SPORTS PSYCHOLOGY

Life itself is a tough competition. Competition means development of a sense of competing with others. In a family we compete with our brothers and sisters, in the playground of our school we compete with our play-mates, in the class-room we compete with our class-mates, as an employee we compete with colleagues, as a businessman we compete with our co-partners, as a nation we compete with other nation. So competition is found every where in each and every sphere of life at each and every age level.

Now the question arises, who are the best competitors? Who all get success in the competition? The answers to these questions are very simple. Only those who develop under the sports - psychology get the success.

Through sports and games, not only children but adults also gain the competitive spirit. And once you develop this spirit, you automatically learn to struggle, to fix-up the goal and to become a winner.

Different Age Levels and Sports Psychology

Age level — 4 year to 5 years

Crawling Competition

At this age level children learn to crawl, Children with competitive spirit crawl faster than the other children.

Snatching Competition

At this age level children snatch things from each other. So the children with competitive spirit actively snatch things from others.

Crying Competition

At this age level if one child is crying, another also starts crying and the child with competitive spirit crises more loudly than other children.

Age level — 6 years to 15 years

Competition in Studies

During this age period children compete in studies.

Competition in Games

Children compete when they play games.

At home children play indoor games also which help in the sharpening of their brains.

Children compete while playing in school children play outdoor games and participate in running races also. So at this age level we see the children with an instinct of competing with others, always win. If we observe minutely by standing in the playground, we will see that all children are not alike. Some give-up in the beginning, some give-up when they get tired but those who play the game till end, they are called the real competitors.

Competition in Other Co-curricular Activities

Generally, those children who are good in sports, they are good in other co-curricular activities also. They actively participate in Debates, Dance and Song competitions.

Age Level – 16 years and above

At this age level, it is clear that competition is a term which go side by side through out our life. Till we are alive we keep on competing with others.

Not only during studies but after finishing our studies when we take-up a job, we see that there is a continuous competition. For example, every doctor competes with other doctors, every lawyer competes with other lawyers and every person competes with other persons and so on.

Thus, all these competitions definitely have a strong base of sports activities with them. A book-worm may and may not be a good competitor but a sportsman definitely goes up higher with strong competitive spirit.

Co-relation between Sports and Competitive Spirit

There is positive co-relation between competitive spirit and sports. In other words, the more he/she is good in sports, the more they have competitive spirit in them. Generally, it is found that at the time of different interviews for different posts the selected candidates have a strong base of sports-psychology. Through this sports psychology only they learn to win their respective goals.

Therefore, it is true to say that through games and sports only we can develop the competitive spirit in the children which definitely pays them in the long run through out their life.